THE FJH
CONTEMPORARY
KEYBOARD
EDITIONS

Piano Album
Thirteen Light and Descriptive Piano Pieces

Late Intermediate/Early Advanced

edited by Helen Marlais

Dimitar Ninov

Dedicated to my son, Nino

Production: Frank and Gail Hackinson
Production Coordinators: Philip Groeber, Isabel Otero Bowen
Cover: Terpstra Design, San Francisco
Cover Painting: White Stroke, 1920, W. Kandinsky
Text Design & Layout: Maritza Cosano Gomez
Engraving: Tempo Music Press, Inc.
Printer: Tempo Music Press, Inc.

ISBN 1-56939-449-0

Copyright © MMV by
THE FJH MUSIC COMPANY INC.
2525 Davie Road, Suite 360
Fort Lauderdale, FL 33317-7424
International Copyright Secured.
All Rights Reserved.   Printed in U.S.A.

THE
F·J·H
MUSIC
COMPANY
INC.

Notes from the Composer

I have always been inspired and challenged by the possibilities of depicting particular images through the abstract art of music. Flip through the pages of my *Piano Album*, and they will introduce you to a gallery of musical pictures. You will "see" the sparrow leaping among the branches of a tree; you will "feel" the melancholy of autumn with its golden leaves falling; and you will "hear" the mischievous gossip spreading around the neighborhood, or the threatening growl of a wolf chasing after his prey in the forest. *Bulgarian Dance* will acquaint you with fascinating rhythms from the folk music of beautiful Bulgaria, and the jingling of *Santa Claus' Sleigh* will remind you of the miraculous atmosphere on a Christmas Evening.

As performers, you will need to have reached a relatively advanced level of proficiency at the piano. Although this album is not designed as a collection of progressive studies for the instrument, the benefits you will reap in terms of piano technique will be enormous, should you decide to perfect your performance of all the pieces. Being keenly interested in the pieces you are playing and with time and practice, you will gradually overcome the technical obstacles and come to enjoy building the character of the piece in terms of dynamics, tempo changes, touch, and feeling. Dear friends, I hope you will spend wonderful hours with the characters and scenes depicted within this collection!

Sincerely,
Dimitar Ninov

About the Composer

Dimitar Ninov was born in Varna, Bulgaria, on May 27, 1963. He graduated from the French Language High School in his native town. In 1987, he entered the State Academy of Music *Pancho Vladigerov* in Sofia, where he earned master's degrees in two majors: Theory of Music (1992) and Composition (1996). Ninov studied composition with one of the most prominent Bulgarian composers, Prof. Alexander Raitchev. His graduation thesis was a Concerto for Clarinet and Orchestra, premiered by the Academic Orchestra in May, 1996.

From 1992-1997, Ninov was employed as a conductor of the children's choir *Bonka Golemanova* in Botevgrad. Between 1994 and 1999, he gave private instruction in harmony, solfège and other disciplines in Sofia, and worked as a composer and arranger in the field of popular music. In 1999, Dimitar Ninov went to the United States to pursue his doctoral studies in composition. He was employed as a teaching assistant in theory of music at the University of South Carolina, and later at the University of Texas at Austin.

In May 2003, Ninov earned his doctorate in composition at the University of Texas with *Spring Symphony*, a three-movement symphony for orchestra. The composer has produced a body of works for orchestra, chamber ensembles, choir, voice, and piano.

A Special Note to Students

Welcome to the exciting world of music written for you during our time! The composer of this collection is someone you could actually speak to and meet! You will discover new sounds and pedal effects, and interesting melodies, rhythms, and harmonies that will be fun to play! You will notice that the pieces in this collection are contrasting in nature—some are energetic, others lyrical—some are sad, others are humorous.

As you explore this book, use your imagination to create your very own interpretation of these wonderful new pieces. The title of each work will give you your first clue as to how to bring the piece to life, and the musical indications (tempo, dynamics, articulation and pedal markings, etc.) will provide a map to guide you through this exciting musical journey.

Enjoy these pieces!

Sincerely,
Helen Marlais

About the Editor

Helen Marlais has given collaborative recitals throughout the U.S. and in Canada, Italy, Germany, Turkey, Hungary, Lithuania, Russia, and China. She is recorded on Gasparo and Centaur record labels, and has performed and given workshops at local, state and national music teachers' conventions, including the National Conference on Keyboard Pedagogy and the National Music Teacher's convention. She is Director of Keyboard Publications for the FJH Music Company and her articles can be read in major keyboard journals.

Dr. Marlais is an associate professor of piano at Grand Valley State University in Grand Rapids, MI. She has also held full-time faculty piano positions at the Crane School of Music, S.U.N.Y. at Potsdam, Iowa State University, and Gustavus Adolphus College.

Table of Contents

The Sparrow

Dimitar Ninov

Allegro e leggiero (♩ = 120-126)

Golden Leaves

Dimitar Ninov

Doloroso e cantabile (♩. = 54)

The Clown

Dimitar Ninov

Ragtime

Dimitar Ninov

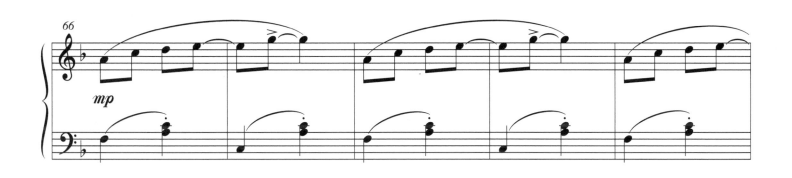

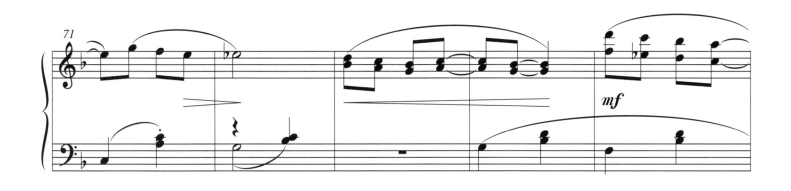

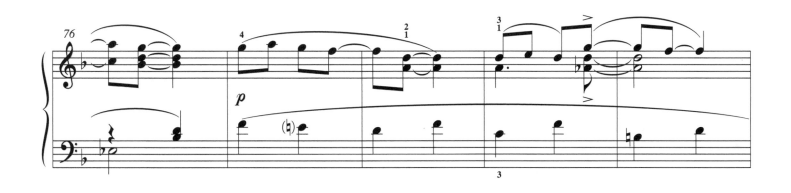

Gossip

Dimitar Ninov

18

Sea World

Dimitar Ninov

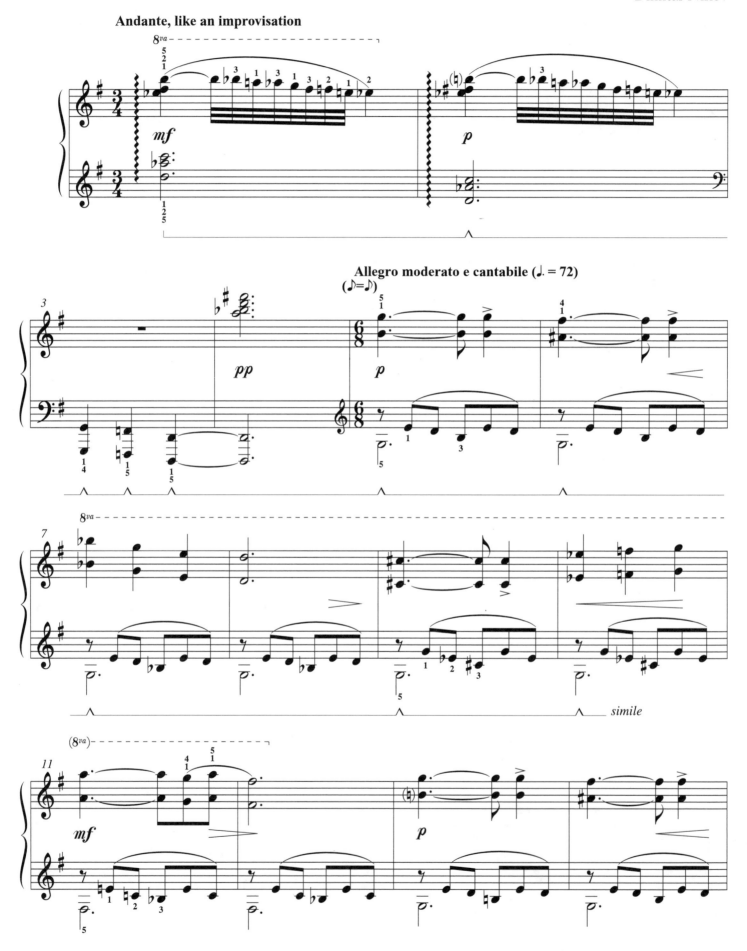

Little Girl

Dimitar Ninov

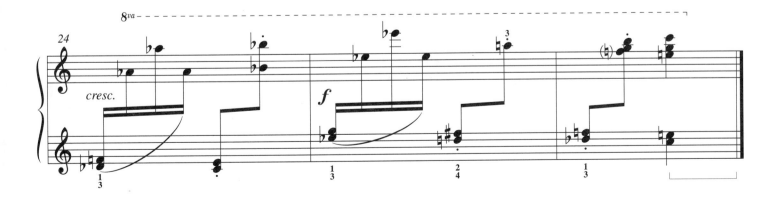

The Wolf

Dimitar Ninov

Solitude

Dimitar Ninov

Excursion

Dimitar Ninov

pedal as before

At the Royal Court

Dimitar Ninov

Bulgarian Dance

Dimitar Ninov

Santa Claus' Sleigh

Dimitar Ninov

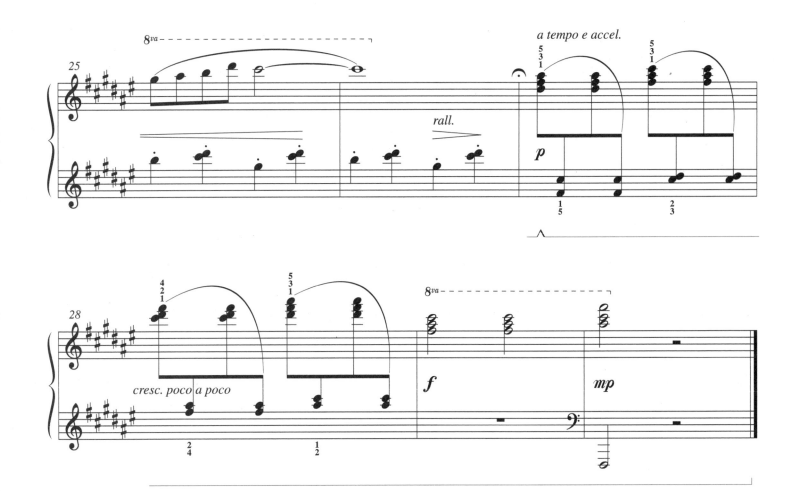